The Romantic Castles of Scotland

by Alec Court

Book Three
Including Stately Homes and Palaces

The scope of this third book of the romantic castles of Scotland has been extended to include palaces and some of the larger stately homes. The reader's attention is drawn to the introduction to Book One where the evolution of the Scottish castle is discussed; it is logical to include palaces and large mansions in a book of this nature, as both are, in fact, further developments of the castle, which in the course of time changed from being a purely defensive building into a residence of the laird, and was adapted to provide more homely comforts.

I

2

3

The village of Scone could be described as the cradle of the Scottish monarchy, for it was in the old palace here that the Scottish kings were crowned on the historic Stone of Scone, a block of red sandstone which had been brought here, probably from Ireland, in the eighth century. Edward I removed the stone to England and it was subsequently placed beneath the Coronation Chair in Westminster Abbey. The present *Palace of Scone (title-page)* dates only from the last century.

Ever since the eleventh century the Brodie family has owned the lands around *Brodie Castle (1)* between Nairn and Forres. Although the castle was burned in 1645 during the campaign of Montrose, most of the older building survived and was incorporated in the rebuilding. The earliest part of the present castle is the tower, dating from the fifteenth century. A feature of the interior is the valuable collection of English and Dutch paintings.

Delgatie Castle (2), two miles north-east of the village of Turriff, in the Deveron Valley, was built between the twelfth and sixteenth centuries. There is a turnpike stair with ninety-seven steps; groined and painted ceilings; arms and armour; and interesting pictures and furnishings.

The castle has associations with Mary Queen of Scots. On the first Saturday of July the Delgatie Shoot is held – by command of James VI in 1584. This is the oldest archery meeting in the United Kingdom. The castle is open by appointment only – no casual callers are admitted.

The Urquhart family has owned *Craigston Castle (3)* ever since it was built at the beginning of the seventeenth century. It conforms to the E-plan and has a most unusual feature in that the two wings are joined four storeys up by an archway and a balcony. The corbelling at the angles of the walls suggests that the original plan conceived angle turrets, but it seems that these were never built. The interior is notable for its fine woodwork and vaulted basements.

The strangely named *Towie-Barclay Castle (4)*, so called to distinguish it from Towie Castle in Strathedon, stands in the parish of Auchterless, some five miles south of Turriff. It dates from the fifteenth century, but at a later period the top two storeys were dismantled, and the exterior now presents a somewhat mixed appearance. The interior is notable for the fine vaulting of the basement and for its minstrels' gallery. The property, the seat of the Barclay family, has now been restored.

5

Leith Hall (5), near the village of Kenneth-mont, is a most charming family home, which, though its architecture spans some 300 years, nevertheless succeeds in presenting a feeling of harmony, so excellently have later additions been matched to the original tower block. The house was begun by one James Leith in the middle of the seventeenth century and consider-ably enlarged a hundred years later by his grandson, John, who used the original turreted tower as the fourth side of a quadrangle, at the four corners of which he constructed two-storeyed buildings. The last major addition was made in the nineteenth century and consisted of a large front hall added to the eastern flank.

At the confluence of the rivers Deveron and Bogie stands *Huntly Castle (6)*, one of the most impressive historical castles in Scotland. The ruins we see here now are those of the building which was begun in the fifteenth century, but there was an earlier Norman castle on the site, built by Duncan, Earl of Fife, the first Laird of Strathbogie. In the time of Bruce the Strathbogie family was dispossessed and the estate given to Sir Adam Gordon of Huntly in Berwickshire. Each of his descendants, styled Lords of Huntly and Dukes of Gordon, was known as 'The Cock of the North'. The principal features of the ruins are the six-storeyed oblong keep with its circular tower and the carved heraldic devices in the stonework.

6

Photograph by kind permission of Aberdeen Tourist Board.

7

Haddo House (7), the ancestral home of the earls and marquesses of Aberdeen, was designed in the Palladian style by William Adam and built in the early 1730s. Structural changes were made in the last century, mainly internal improvements and the provision of an internal staircase. The stone steps seen in the photograph lead directly to the reception rooms on the first floor.

In recent years Haddo House has become well known through the activities of the Haddo House Choral Society which has its headquarters here. The chapel, seen on the right, has an important place in the musical life of the centre; it was built in 1881 to the design of Sir George Street.

Druminnor (8), originally called Castle Forbes, was the seat of the Forbes clan before they moved to Keig some eight miles to the south-east, where the present Castle Forbes is now situated. Druminnor dates from the second half of the sixteenth century but includes part of a fifteenth-century fortified house. Although it sadly fell into neglect, the castle was bought by the daughter of Lord Semphill, a member of the clan, and she set about restoring it to its former grandeur. The building stands on a sloping site and thus there are two extra storeys on the south front. The rooms in the lower storeys here are vaulted and in one of them there appears over the chimney-piece the inscription A HAPPY ROOM 144 I.R., which is believed to refer to James II. The Forbes and Gordon clans were constantly feuding with each other, and it is chronicled that fifteen of the latter were killed while being entertained at a banquet in Druminnor.

Dating from the beginning of the sixteenth century, *Craig Castle (9)* is essentially an ancient L-shaped stronghold to which a more modern residence has been added. Originally the castle had parapets and a flat roof, but gabled roofs were superimposed a century after its inception. Strong walls, which in places are two metres thick, and gun-loops testify to the fact that the castle was intended as a fortress for the Gordons of Craig. There is interesting heraldic panelling and the hall has a minstrels' gallery.

The beautifully preserved ruins of *Tolquhon Castle (10)* bear witness to the skill of its builders. The original keep was built by the Preston family early in the fifteenth century, and the rest between 1584 and 1589 by William Forbes, whose family had acquired the property by marriage. The entrance is flanked by two round towers and surmounted by a finely carved heraldic panel giving the dates of the commencement and completion of the main building.

There are a considerable number of castellated houses in Scotland, but few are more attractive and worthy of attention than *Balbithan (11)*, a laird's home, the earliest part of which dates from the first part of the seventeenth century.

Balbithan is a typical L-shaped building, but there are architectural differences between the two wings, and the stair tower pre-dates both.

The main part of the mansion was built by William Chalmers between 1660 and 1670 at a time when the style of the tower-house was

losing favour and the architecture of the Restoration was more fashionable. Although the corner turrets and steep gables of the typical tower-house are present, the level of the roof has been apparently lowered so that it is no longer possible to gain access to the turrets at the angles of the building.

Pitcaple Castle (12), an excellent example of a Z-plan tower-house, is situated to the north of the main Aberdeen–Inverness highway. The oldest part dates from the second half of the fifteenth century, but the major part of the building took place in the early seventeenth century. Reconstruction was undertaken about a hundred years ago. Many famous figures of Scottish and English history visited Pitcaple, among them James IV, Mary Queen of Scots and Charles II.

Glenbuchat (13), one of the most romantic ruined fortresses in Scotland, is situated on a knoll close to the confluences of the rivers Don and Buchat. It was built at the end of the sixteenth century by John Gordon and his second wife, Helen Carnegie, as is shown by the inscription over the entrance: 'Nothing on arth remains bot fame. John Gordone – Helen Carnegie 1590'. Originally there was another and longer inscription in the form of a metaphysical poem on the staircase, but this has

now disappeared. The castle, built on the Z-plan, has one particularly unusual feature – the two stair-turrets are supported by squinch arches and not, as is more usual, by corbelling. Of the long line of the Gordons of Glenbuchat, the most celebrated was the last laird, also named John, but popularly called 'Old Glenbuchat of the '45'. He had, in fact, taken part in the 1715 Uprising and was already sixty-eight when the '45 Rebellion began. Nevertheless, he raised a small army and marched with the clans to Derby and all the way back to Culloden. After the defeat of Prince Charles's forces, John Gordon managed to disguise himself and flee to Norway and subsequently to France where he died penniless.

There could be few finer examples of the architectural style favoured in the late fifteenth and the sixteenth centuries, and popularly called 'Scottish Baronial', than *Castle Fraser (14),* some twenty miles to the west of Aberdeen. To the fifteenth-century keep a Z-planned fortress and a round seven-storeyed tower were added in the late sixteenth century. The title of Lord Fraser, given by Charles I in 1633, became extinct in 1720.

Balfluig Castle (15) stands in the fertile valley of the River Don, a mile to the west of Alford. Dating from the middle of the sixteenth century, the castle is a good example of a modestly sized

tower-house on the L-plan.

Among the interesting features of this charmingly restored building are a little watch-chamber at the head of the staircase, vaulted basements and a prison beneath the stairs.

The five towers of *Fyvie Castle (16)* enshrine five centuries of Scottish history, each being built by one of the five families who owned the castle – the Prestons, the Meldrums, the Setons, the Gordons and the Leiths. The oldest part dates from the thirteenth century and it is now probably the grandest example of Scottish Baronial architecture. The castle today houses an exceptionally important collection of portraits including works by Ramsay, Batoni, Raeburn and Gainsborough.

Perched high overlooking the main coastal road running south from Aberdeen is *Muchalls Castle (17)*, an E-planned building of the early seventeenth century. The castle is noteworthy for the splendour of the heraldic plaster ceilings of the Great Hall and other principal rooms. The castle belonged to the Frasers until 1614, but after Andrew Fraser fell into disgrace it passed to the Burnetts and is still privately owned.

To the north of Fettercairn stretches a curious earthwork known as the 'Deer Dyke', which

15

once enclosed a royal hunting-ground. Near its western end stands *Fasque House (18)*, a castellated mansion built in 1809 on the site of an earlier castle. In 1828 the house was acquired by the father of William Ewart Gladstone, who forty years later became Prime Minister.

Kisimul Castle (19) stands on a rocky islet in Castlebay on the Island of Barra in the Outer Hebrides. It is believed that there was a castle here as early as the eleventh century, but the present building, which was restored about forty years ago, is of fifteenth-century date. The bare walls of the medieval castle now conceal a more modern private residence.

The Island of Mull, the second largest of the Inner Hebrides, is separated from the mainland by the Firth of Lorne. At its north-eastern tip, on Duart Point, stands the restored *Duart Castle (20)*, the ancestral seat of the Macleans. The name Duart is derived from Gaelic words meaning 'Black Height', a reference to the rock on which the castle is situated. There is a rock just off the shore called 'Lady Rock' on which, according to legend, one of the Macleans left his wife, wishing to get rid of her. Fortunately, this dramatic story has a happy ending, for she was rescued by fishermen and her evil spouse was eventually slain.

From *Torosay Castle (21)* on the Isle of Mull one can enjoy fine views over the Firth of Lorne and along the coast, even as far as Ben Nevis. The house, in the Scottish Baronial style, was designed by David Bryce during the last century and the gardens were laid out by Sir Robert Lorimer in the fashionable Italianate style of the period, with many life-sized statues. Torosay,

which is open to the public from Easter to the
autumn, has family portraits by leading artists
and wildlife paintings and drawings by, among
others, Landseer and Sir Peter Scott, as well as old
photographs of the days of sail.

All that remains of the once-proud *Finavon
Castle (22)* is a ruined tower which was probably
built in the sixteenth century but was constructed
above an earlier fortification. The castle, which
was the home of the Earls of Crawford, is
situated about five miles to the north-east of
Forfar. The remains, scanty though they are,
bear testimony to the fact that the castle must
have been a mighty fortress from the fourteenth
century when the Lindsay family first acquired
the estate, which is in the midst of a thickly
wooded area, once part of a royal forest.

Huntingtower Castle (23) was originally called
the Castle of Ruthven, and it was in this
stronghold that the adolescent James VI was held
prisoner by a number of Scottish nobles. In 1600
James revenged himself on his abductors and
ruled that the name of Ruthven should never
again be borne by people or places. The castle
was given to the Murrays, later Dukes of Atholl,
and renamed Huntingtower. The solid-looking
building was originally two towers, one built in
the early fifteenth century and the other nearly
200 years later. Formerly they were joined only
by a narrow passage at parapet level. The space

between the towers is known as 'Maiden's Leap', where, according to legend, the daughter of one of the Ruthvens jumped across the gap in order to escape being found by her parents with her secret lover!

Dating from the sixteenth century, the noble ruin of *Elcho Castle (24)* stands close to the banks of the Tay, a mile to the north of the village of Rhynd. The building, four storeys high, has four projecting towers with splayed gun-loops. It is now in the care of the Department of the Environment. The castle was the seat of the Earls of Wemyss, the first Earl having been created in 1633 by Charles I when he was crowned at Holyrood.

Drummond Castle (25), which has had a long and chequered history, stands on a hillock some two miles north-west of Muthill in Perth. A seat of the Earls of Ancaster, the castle was built at the end of the fifteenth century and is today kept as a museum, the modern house being on an adjacent site. During the Civil War the castle was besieged and partially destroyed and further demolition was carried out in 1745 by the Duchess of Perth, a Jacobite, who was fearful that the castle might by captured by the Hanoverians. Some rebuilding has subsequently been carried out. The most notable feature of the estate is the magnificent gardens, first laid out by the second Earl of Perth in the seventeenth century. About

140 years ago the gardens were considerably remodelled and enlarged and now contain many rare plants and trees. A noteworthy feature is a sundial dated 1630 which registers the time in most of the chief cities of Europe.

Falkland, in the ancient kingdom of Fife, has been a royal burgh for hundreds of years. *Falkland Palace (26 and front cover)*, now in the care of the National Trust for Scotland, was probably begun by James III on the site of an older castle, and it was considerably enlarged by the succeeding Stuarts who used it principally as a hunting-lodge. The interior is notable for the chapel, once a banqueting hall, which has a fine ceiling and an unusual oak screen. In the 'King's Room' James V, who had been imprisoned in the palace as a boy by the Earl of Angus, is believed to have died shortly after hearing the news that at Linlithgow his wife had given birth to a daughter, later to become the ill-fated Mary Queen of Scots. Mary was a frequent visitor to Falkland, which is a good example of the French Renaissance style. In 1654 the east wing was burnt down while Cromwell's troops were billeted in the building, but in recent years the remaining ranges have been carefully restored and are of great historical interest.

Inveraray Castle (27), the seat of the Duke of Argyll, was begun in 1743 to the design of Roger Morris and completed after his death by John Adam. It is one of the earliest and one of the largest neo-Gothic mansions in the country and

is justly famous for the comprehensive collection of furniture, tapestries, paintings and armoury which since 1953 have been on view to the public. When the house was first built the whole of the township of Inveraray, which was situated near the former keep, was rebuilt on a new site nearby. The castle has been twice damaged by fire; the most recent occasion was in 1976, but

27

fortunately complete restoration has taken place.

Dunimarle Castle (28) is yet another example of a castellated house built on the site of a former fortified mansion. It occupies an elevated position to the west of Culross in Fife. Legend has it that the original castle was the scene of the murder of Lady Macduff and her children, but Castle Hill at Cupar also claims this dubious distinction. The castle has a good collection of paintings and porcelain as well as some excellent glass from Bohemia.

Of the four royal palaces in Scotland one is at *Linlithgow (29)*, the former county town of West Lothian. The Normans had a palace here in the twelfth century but it was James I of Scotland who in the fifteenth century initiated the building of the palace which we know today. Over the gateway are the insignia of the Orders of the Thistle, the Garter, St Michael and the Golden Fleece. Most of the buildings date from the fifteenth century but the north side was not added until some eighty years later. In the quadrangle stands a fountain of the time of James V and a copy of this can be seen outside

Holyrood House in Edinburgh. The usual domestic rooms include a kitchen with an imposing fireplace, and a Great Hall, some one hundred feet long, which is also known as the Lyon Hall. This has a finely restored triple chimney-piece. The royal apartments include the room in which Mary Queen of Scots was born and, at the head of the spiral stair, Queen Margaret's Bower, where the Queen is supposed to have awaited the return of James VI from the battlefield of Flodden.

In medieval days Blackness, situated on the southern shore of the Firth of Forth, was a flourishing seaport, and *Blackness Castle (30)* was an important fortress. It was built in the fifteenth century and became royal property when its principal use was as a prison. In the seventeenth century captured Covenanters were incarcerated here, and the importance of the castle can be gauged by the fact that after the Acts of Union in 1707 it was reported to be one of only four castles which were to be fully garrisoned, although the historical accuracy of this report has been challenged.

Three miles to the south of Abercorn, where the first Scottish bishopric was founded in the seventh century, stands *The Binns (31)*, the ancestral home of the Dalyells. Although the estate is documented as long ago as the fourteenth century, the present castle is largely of the early seventeenth century. A feature of the mansion, which was presented in 1944 to the National Trust for Scotland and is open to the public, is a number of beautifully moulded plaster ceilings dating from the earliest days of the building.

Dumbarton Castle (32), an Ancient Monument, occupies a commanding position on a hill crowned by twin basaltic peaks. Most of the old buildings have gone, but a gateway dating from the twelfth century and a sundial, reputed to have been a gift of Mary Queen of Scots, are still to be seen. Mary left the castle in 1548 to journey to France. Dumbarton was the capital of the Kingdom of Strathclyde for at least 500 years before the eleventh century and there was certainly a stone castle on the present site in medieval times. The view from the castle rock of

Glasgow and the Clyde is of fascinating interest.

The Palace of Holyrood (33), the official Scottish residence of the Sovereign, was originally the Abbey of the Holy Rood, or Cross, founded by King David I in 1128. It became a royal residence during the reign of James IV and he or his son built the northern tower and Queen Mary's apartments which still stand today. Serious fires in 1543 and 1650 destroyed much of the buildings then existing, and although Cromwell had begun reconstruction, it was Charles II who was responsible for the building as we know it today. Its architecture owes much to French inspiration. Of the Abbey Church, which dates largely from the eleventh century and is sometimes known as the Chapel Royal, there remain only the ruins of the roofless nave. Here many of the Scottish kings were married and here Charles I was crowned. In the Royal Vault lie the remains of several members of the

Scottish royalty. The interior of the Palace is of great historical interest. The State Apartments, which are occupied by the Sovereign when in residence in Edinburgh, contain many rare furnishings, tapestries and paintings, and the visitor is shown the rooms occupied by the ill-fated Mary Queen of Scots and her husband, Lord Darnley. A brass plate in the supper-room

marks the spot where Mary's Italian secretary, Rizzio, is said to have been murdered.

Hopetoun House (34), formerly the seat of the Earls of Hopetoun and now of the Marquis of Linlithgow, stands by the village of Abercorn to the west of Edinburgh and overlooks the Forth Estuary. It is one of the most impressive mansions in the whole of Scotland and is open to the public at certain times. The formal gardens, which were laid out on the model of Versailles, are a feature of the estate. The house itself was begun at the very end of the seventeenth century by Sir

William Bruce of Kinross, who was also engaged in the reconstruction of the Palace of Holyroodhouse. Subsequently the mansion was enlarged by William Adam and his sons. The beautifully symmetrical classical exterior is matched by some superb rooms containing priceless paintings, among which are masterpieces by Rembrandt, Van Dyck, Titian and Rubens. Visitors to Hopetoun can see in the park herds of fallow and red deer and a flock of the renowned St Kilda sheep.

Now an Ancient Monument, *Newark Castle (35)* is a witness to the importance of Port Glasgow, originally named Newark, before dredging of the Clyde opened up sea-borne trade into Glasgow itself. Newark Castle is typical of the strongholds built in the late sixteenth and early seventeenth centuries. Although now overshadowed by industrial development the castle is well preserved and has a fine courtyard and hall. Port Glasgow was founded early in the second half of the seventeenth century; its Customs House was built in 1710, and James Watt designed the first graving dock, which was built in 1762. Until trading ships were able to reach Glasgow, the port had a flourishing trade in tobacco and timber with America, and although this declined in the nineteenth century, the Industrial Revolution brought renewed prosperity in the form of shipbuilding.

Haggs Castle (36), an excellent example of an L-shaped house is situated in the suburb of Pollockshaws in the western part of the City of Glasgow. Although the building has been considerably altered and restored, the castle was probably built towards the end of the sixteenth century for the powerful Maxwell family of Pollock. The ancient kitchen on the ground floor houses a fireplace some nineteen feet wide and five feet deep, and there is another fine fireplace in the hall on the first floor.

About ten miles to the south-east of Glasgow, *Bothwell Castle (37)* stands on a hill above the River Clyde. Originally built in the thirteenth century, the castle, which was a stronghold of the Douglas clan, has had an eventful history. It suffered partial destruction after the Battle of Bannockburn; some restoration took place in the first half of the fourteenth century, but it was again attacked, and it was not until the last years of that century that the third Earl of Douglas rendered it again habitable. The great round tower, which is modelled on that of Concy in France, and much of the outer walls, nearly fifteen feet thick and sixty feet high in places, are still in fair condition. The whole structure has

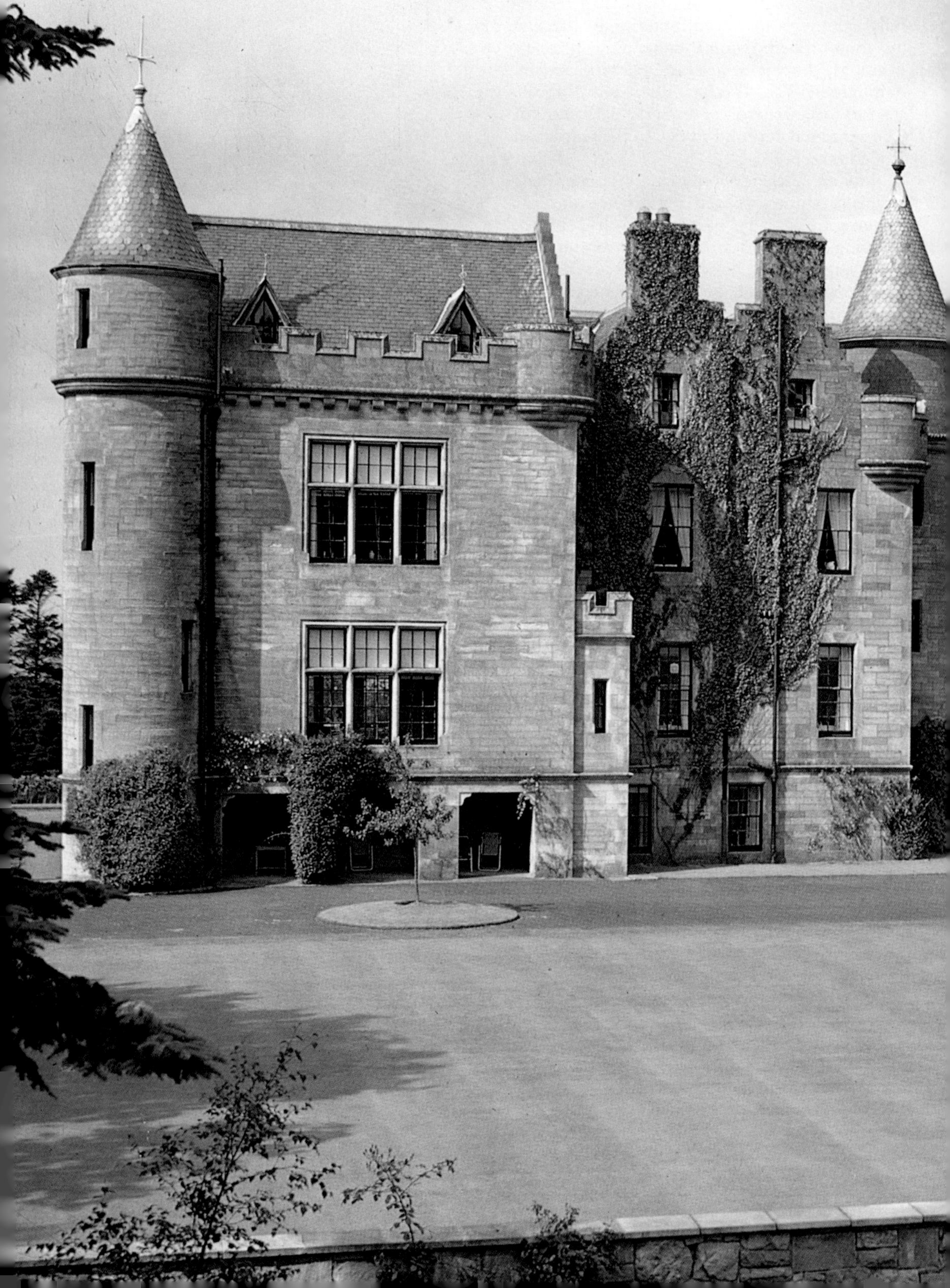

been designated an Ancient Monument and is in the care of the Department of the Environment. Sir Walter Scott wrote *Young Lochinvar* while staying in a house which had been built from material taken from the castle.

Glenapp Castle (38), the seat of the Earl of Inchcape, lies just to the south of Ballantrae at the head of the beautiful glen of the same name which is traversed by the main road to Stranraer. Glenapp Castle is an excellent example of the Scottish Baronial mansion, but is more widely known for its delightful gardens, in which grow a profusion of azaleas, rhododendrons and many other plants and shrubs. In Glen App, too, stands a little church which has been restored to the memory of Elsie Mackay who was lost in a plane while crossing the Atlantic in 1928.

Whenever one strays from the mainland of the west of Scotland and visits one of the delightful islands, one is constantly reminded of the distant past when the Norsemen raided these shores. The Island of Bute was in the forefront of these raids, and it is believed by some that *Rothesay Castle (39)* was founded by a Norwegian king at the end of the eleventh century. More certain is that the castle was seized by the Norsemen in the thirteenth century when the present fortress was built. It suffered greatly during the troubled times which followed and was burned by Cromwell's soldiers in the seventeenth century. The remains consist of a strong curtain-wall surrounding a courtyard, the whole encircled by a moat. Rothesay Castle figures in Scott's *The Fair Maid of Perth*.

Mellerstain (40) is situated about seven miles to the north of Kelso, in Berwickshire. It is a fine castellated mansion dating from 1725; it is a seat of the Earls of Haddington, and is open to the public at certain times. This magnificent Georgian house was designed by William Adam and

completed by his son Robert, who was responsible not only for the main part of the building but also for the splendid interior, where he used much coloured plasterwork. Perhaps the most interesting rooms are the Library, with a fine ceiling, and the original dining-room, which boasts a fireplace incorporating carved figures of War and Peace. The Great Gallery houses a collection of costumes, books and silverware. Of particular interest are the gardens, laid out in the Italianate manner of the period, which are complemented by an ornamental lake.

The story of *Abbotsford (41)* is really the story of Sir Walter Scott. Born in Edinburgh in 1771, Scott became a legal official, and continued to fulfil his duties until nearing the end of his life. His literary output was enormous, first of poetry and later, when Byron was in the ascendancy, of long historical prose romances. After his early successes Scott took up residence in 1804 at Ashiestiel on the River Tweed and some six years later bought a small farm at Cartley Hole, near Melrose, and began to convert the cottage on it into the mansion of Abbotsford, a task which was to take about seven years. Here Scott set about establishing a collection of historical relics, some purchased and others received as gifts, which was to make his last home a veritable treasure-house. In 1820 he was made a baronet, but a few years later found himself in debt to the tune of over £120,000, a mighty sum indeed in those days. The tragedy was the result of the failure of two printing and publicity firms, Ballantyne and Constable, in which Scott was a partner. With commendable spirit Scott set about the task of clearing his debts by more writing, and although he paid off more than half, ill-health finally took toll of him, and after a brief visit to Italy he returned to Abbotsford for the last time and died on 21 September 1832. The house is a monument to its builder and owner.

It would be difficult to find a more complete contrast to the classical architecture of Mellerstain than *Traquair House (42)*, reputed to be the oldest inhabited house in Scotland. The oldest part of this mansion is the tower, which is believed to date from the tenth century, but the main block was built in the seventeenth century by the first Earl of Traquair and wings were added later in the same century. Before this time Traquair had famous visitors in the persons of Mary Queen of Scots and her husband, Lord Darnley, who stayed in the 'King's Room' in the tower. There are a number of relics of the ill-fated Mary still to be seen in the house. Perhaps the most fascinating feature of Traquair House is the mystery surrounding the locked gates at the end of the main avenue – the 'Steekit Yetts' as they are called. There are two explanations: the first and more probable is that the gates were closed by the seventh Earl in 1796 after his wife's funeral procession had passed through them, and he vowed that they would never again be opened until another countess came to Traquair. There has, alas, never been another, and so the gates remain locked. The second explanation is that favoured by Sir Walter Scott, namely that the gates were locked after a visit by the Young

42

Pretender in 1745, the Earl swearing that they would be unlocked only when a Stuart should become king.

Dean Castle (43), home of the Boyd family, Lords of Kilmarnock, dates from about 1360 when the main tower or keep was built to defend the lands of Kilmarnock. After falling into ruin in the eighteenth century, the castle was restored by the eighth Lord Howard de Walden between 1908 and 1946. In 1975 the castle was presented as a gift to the town of Kilmarnock by the ninth Lord Howard de Walden, together with a vast collection of arms, armour, tapestries and early musical instruments.

Vanbrugh designed *Floors Castle (back cover)*, one of the grandest houses in the whole of Scotland. It stands in an extensive park by the River Tweed. A holly tree on the estate is reputed to mark the spot where James II was killed when a cannon blew up during the siege of Roxburgh in 1460. Vanbrugh's grand design was apparently not sufficent for the Dukes of Roxburgh, and in the last century the house was remodelled by Playfair. The ornamental 'Golden Gates' and flanking lodges at the end of the main avenue were built as recently as 1929.

43